Jukeboxes & Jackalopes

A Photographic Companion to Wyoming Bars & Backways

Julianne Couch & Ronald K. Hansen

Published by the
Wyoming State Historical Society
P.O. Box 247
Wheatland, WY 82201

ISBN 978-0-9842055-0-9

Set in Horley Old Style
Designed by Horse Creek Studio

Printed in the United States of America

Dedicated to
Alice James, FDR, William Boyd, Irma,
and the people of
Wyoming – past, present, and future

Acknowledgements

We wish to thank the
Wyoming State Historical Society
for the publication of this book, also the
University of Wyoming's College of Arts & Sciences
and the Wyoming Arts Council
for their generous financial support
of this project.

Contents

(continued on following page)

Contents

Preface

One of Wyoming's most successful politicians campaigned every four years in every Wyoming county. Unlike some of us who were not as successful, he did not begin his visits to each town by going to the newspaper office, the radio station, or even the downtown café. He started out in the neighborhood bars. The campaign style had its benefits–he didn't have to show up during regular daytime office hours or during the 10 o'clock or 3 o'clock coffee breaks. In some of the smaller places, there hardly was a choice of stops. As another traveler once said, "A town in Wyoming consists of a post office, a gas station, and a bar." And, sometimes in recent decades, rural routes supplanted some of the post offices.

In the past couple of decades, many Wyoming newspapers became chain-owned, radio stations run by automation from two time zones away, and coffee places operated by national caffeine-distribution networks. Booms came and went; busts decimated lots of small towns. Even dispensaries of liquor have evolved, with the convention hotel providing an all-purpose stop for the thirsty traveler. As generational tastes changed, once thriving taverns are closed and boarded.

Despite all of the changes, in Wyoming, some distinctive, classic watering spots still serve up a cold one or a bracer against the winter winds. In some cases, the exteriors seem little changed since the end of Prohibition. In others, the accumulation of artifacts hanging from the walls or decorating the back bar continue to accumulate as the decades roll onward. Like brands–those burned symbols on the flank of a cow–each of the bars pictured in this book has its own identifying brand–the flat-top bar stools, the leather bar edge, the brass rail, silver dollar inlays, or hunks of jade. The jukeboxes and the jackalopes of the book title. Even the names hint at their uniqueness.

(continued on following page)

Author Julianne Couch wrote of her impressions of many of these legendary places in *Jukeboxes & Jackalopes: A Wyoming Bar Journey*. In this volume, through the skilled photographic eye of her fellow bar tourist Ronald K. Hansen, one can see why so many of those drinking establishments inspired the stories, entertained the great story-tellers, the dancers, the singers, the lovers—and held communities of hard-working men and women together through drought and cold winters. As each photograph shows, each bar—like its owner—has a distinctive look and a unique feel. These snapshots of Wyoming bars catch these moments in time and give you, the reader and viewer, the flavor of life in what may be one of the last unpretentious, locally patronized institutions in many Wyoming towns. Welcome to the photo essays by Ronald K. Hansen and captions by Julianne Couch. On each page are pictures that may tell lots of stories of the thousands those places might tell us. Until bars can talk, these photographs will keep some of the legends alive—and maybe even invite us in for a cold one.

Phil Roberts

Introduction

To see weather conditions before setting out on a Wyoming road trip, we hop on the internet and consult the Wyoming Department of Transportation's Webcam site. WYDOT has provided these omniscient eyeballs so we can view the road from home, gripping the computer mouse instead of the steering wheel. Every few minutes we see a refreshed view of thundering trucks, blowing snow, or elk on the move and decide whether to stay or go. One Webcam near our home in Laramie shows the stretch of road between Vedauwoo and the notorious 8,600-foot summit on I-80. That Webcam site is called The Tavern. It is named for the Summit Tavern, once a welcome stopping point along the old Lincoln Highway that lived to see I-80 constructed and then went up in flames some 25 years ago.

The Summit Tavern was a child of the Lincoln Highway and the engine problem – the desire to go and the necessity to stop. If we'd lived in Wyoming long before I-80 supplanted the old Lincoln Highway, we might have sputtered in a '28 Dodge quarter-ton to the highest point of the old road and rested at the Summit Tavern, we taking in beer, the Dodge's radiator taking in water.

Today near the old Tavern site, a bust of Abraham Lincoln looms over travelers passing the I-80 Summit Visitor Center, which is decidedly not a bar. I wish I'd been in Wyoming before I-80, during the days when Abe Lincoln's highway took people across the

country at a relaxed pace. I like to imagine Abe's omniscient spirit accompanying travelers along his road, telling tales of horizontal blizzards and sun dogs, driving rains and mud bogs. He could have recalled the time Gene Krupa's band played in the dance hall at the Elk Mountain Hotel, between gigs in Denver and Salt Lake City. He could have reminisced about the bar in Opal, where splintered plywood now cloaks the ghosts of bar fights past. And Pete's Roc N Rye in Evanston must have been a hopping place in the Lincoln Highway's day too, but now it is slowly sinking back into the earth.

Although we missed the glory days of some Wyoming watering holes, we've been fortunate to visit close to 70 other such welcoming spots around the state. We regret missing many other wonderful bars and communities and not revisiting those bars that have changed hands since our original trip. We don't have to regret missing the Longbranch Saloon in Hawk Springs because we were lucky enough to visit before it went up in flames in 2007. The owners plan to rebuild and we hope they have as much success as did the Old Corral in Centennial, its shiny gift store and peeled-bark furniture now a palimpsest over the charming, ramshackle saloon. Other bars in Wyoming have met their final fates or at least changed hands and names several times since we visited. The landscapes that the bars punctuate are changing too, because the current energy boom has altered the sky and the water and the earth that compose the place and because the large ranches that preserved the place's texture are now quilted with subdivisions and ranchettes.

Nostalgic preoccupation with pre-interstate roadways, small town bars, and unpolluted landscapes may strike some as naive. Note that the word nostalgia is derived from a Greek word meaning to return home. We may not be able to turn back the clock to the days of thriving small towns and clear skies, but we can look into these bars and landscapes with eyes as documentary as an internet Webcam and refresh our view of this place we call home.

A Photographic Note

"Hi! We're on a bar tour of Wyoming." With that greeting from Julianne, we began most of our bar visits. The photography for this book would for the most part not have been possible without the very gracious permission and acceptance of bar patrons, bar owners, and bartenders.

Almost without exception, the Wyoming landscapes, bar exteriors, and interiors were shot hand held. To achieve the candid, warm nature of Wyoming's drinking establishments, no electronic flash was used. Some of the darker interiors required very high ISO settings to photograph successfully, and the resulting photographs exhibit various levels of digital noise. All of the photography was taken with Nikon D70 and Nikon D200 digital cameras in Nikon Electronic Format NEF (RAW).

One of the important concepts of this project was to depict how these social oases relate to their surrounding environments. At first glance most seem to look inward, ignoring those surroundings; however, upon closer examination, many are reflections instead. Saloon walls are covered with local cattle brands; mounted fish, deer, elk, and antelope heads; historical and contemporary photographs; and of course, spirits advertising. Original murals adorn walls, and paintings from local patrons cover ceiling tiles. Display cases contain freeze-dried rattlesnakes, original wood carvings, Native American and Western artifacts. We have included photographic landscapes to visually anchor these social communities into their encompassing physical environments.

Mike Vinich poses in front of the Tiffany back bar. The Union Bar has been in the Vinich family for more than 40 years, many of whom have stood sentry behind the bar.

It is well known as a meeting place for working folks and as a shrine to popular politicians such as President John F. Kennedy. Proprietor and Purple Heart recipient Mike Vinich was Kennedy's friend harkening back to their service in World War II. Vinich was part of the delegation when Wyoming's vote secured Kennedy's nomination at the Democratic convention in 1960. Designed for use by local coal miners and other male patrons, the front bar features a handy – but no longer used – urinal trough.

Svilar's Bar, Hudson

The bar at Svilar's Restaurant is a destination for some, but for others it is a place to wait for a table to open in the dining area. Svilar's is best known for steaks and prime rib. Some diners are most fond of the appetizers that come with each meal. The salad, the relish plate, the ravioli, and the sarma (cabbage rolls) – reflecting the area's multi-ethnic heritage – can leave little room for the main course. Although the restaurant is regionally popular and reservations are suggested, the ambiance is typically Wyoming: laid back and unpretentious, with diners in jeans and work boots mingling with those in dressier attire.

The southern Wind River Mountains as seen from the Upper Green River Basin in Sublette County.

Green River Bar, Daniel

Since 1899, the Green River Bar has sheltered area residents from blizzards. In modern times it has provided an entertaining family hangout, a place to cash paychecks, sing Karaoke, watch Western movies, and even borrow books without a membership from the Joe Hausen Library. Joe was an avid reader who loaded his overflow books onto bookshelves in the bar. He's now gone but his library lives on, and books come and go on the honor system.

Dry Creek Saloon, aka Bill Store & Bill Yacht Club, Bill

Bill the town (population 1) was named for several gentlemen named Bill whose property cornered at about this spot. Locals say the Bill Store became the Bill Yacht Club after a truck carrying carnival goods toppled on the highway, spilling out a little boat that was part of a childrens' ride. Today the bar is known as the Dry Creek Saloon and caters heavily to the railroad workers at the Bill camp. Those workers are part of the human infrastructure that supports mining of Powder River coal.

The Tavern, Fort Laramie

The building that houses this tavern and restaurant, until recently known as *The Tavern*, is reputed to have once stood on the grounds of Fort Laramie. At various times it has also offered rooms for rent in the top floor of the building. The ground level holds the restaurant, and the bar is in the building's basement.

Fort Laramie Tavern, Fort Laramie

Many Hollywood films about Western emigration show weary pioneers straggling across the Oregon Trail and finding relief at well-stocked Fort Laramie. The location was born Fort William in 1834 then later renamed Fort John. It became a military post in 1849 and was given its present name. A treaty signed at the fort in 1868 gave Indians the rights to land north of the Platte River.

Fort Laramie Saloon, Fort Laramie

The treaty to the land was to be good "so long as grass shall grow and water flow." But when Gen. Custer marched his Seventh Cavalry through the area in 1874 and noticed gold in the Black Hills, the short-lived treaty was broken.

The town of Fort Laramie stands just a few miles from the historic fort, which is operated by the National Park Service. The town, and its bars, are popular stopping-off points for bikers traveling to the motorcycle rally in Sturgis, South Dakota.

A knowledgeable geologist could speculate that the Hartville Uplift is a good spot to search for copper and iron. The Uplift area is the location of the Spanish Diggings, quarries where Indians found materials to make projectile points and tools but which were misidentified by local settlers as early Spanish diggings for gold. The area is crossed by the Oregon Trail, and its presence is still visible today in the form of wagon ruts worn into the sandstone near Guernsey.

Miners & Stockmans Bar, Hartville

The Miners and Stockmans Bar in Hartville is reputed to contain the oldest back bar in Wyoming, which was shipped from Germany to Fort Laramie and brought to Hartville after the fort closed.

Mint Bar, Sheridan

The Mint Bar is a destination in itself in this town that blends the traditional western life with a steady flow of tourists and wealthy newcomers. The Mint Bar was established in 1907 and has seen both Prohibition and backroom gambling come and go. Its walls are an art gallery of photos from rodeos and ranch life. Its furnishings and other elements of decor could win awards. The outdoor sign with a cowboy on a bucking bronc is one of the most photographed objects in the state.

Eden Bar, Eden

The Eden Valley lies in the sparsely populated northern Red Desert, on the western edge of the Jack Morrow Hills. The Oregon and Bridger trails pass just to the north and west.

The Eden Bar sprouted up along with other life-sustaining elements when irrigation came to the Eden Valley in 1907. That's when the Carey Act allowed settlers 160 acres of federal land for 50¢ per acre and $30 per acre for water rights. A chalkboard behind the bar keeps everyone informed of birthdays, anniversaries, and other occasions for celebration in this farming and ranching community of about 400 residents.

The Old Buckhorn Bar & Parlor, Laramie

The Buckhorn Bar, housed in one of Laramie's oldest buildings, is on the National Register of Historic Places. It is widely famous for the bullet hole in the mirror behind the bar, shot there from outside in the 1970s. A goal post from UW's War Memorial Stadium was hoisted up by elated football fans after a Cowboy victory over BYU in 1999. Several photographs and shrines commemorate longtime bar patrons who've passed on. The Parlor Bar is upstairs; the "Buckhorn Roll" is a popular way to go down the stairs quickly.

Bud's Bar, Laramie

Laramie is composed of distinct areas including West Laramie, where the Wyoming Territorial Prison stands, and the West Side, home to Bud's Bar. The bar is a popular Saturday hangout for sports fans, and the mascot pony "Cowboy Joe" often stops in after Wyoming Cowboy football games. Generations of patrons have enjoyed toasting under the mounted trout at this "local's" bar.

Double Shot Bar, Rock River

Other than Laramie, Rock River is the only incorporated town in Albany County. The town lies just south of Fort Fetterman Road, once a stage and freighting route connecting the southern trails with the Oregon and Bozeman trail routes at Fort Fetterman. These days, locals use the Fetterman Road as a route to recreation in the Laramie Range. That is, when they aren't occupied shooting games of pool at the Double Shot Bar. A sign above the bar quotes an unattributed verse: "Let no one say and say it to your shame / that all was Beauty here before you came."

Dorothy is a lifelong resident of Superior, a mining town established in the early 1900s. The Canyon Bar, which she owns, has been around since the town's early days. If the bar could talk, it could tell about the boom and bust of several mining districts and corresponding neighborhoods formed around A Mine, B Mine, C Mine, D Mine, W Mine, and the Clark Mine. Other districts included White City and Copenhagen. The Canyon Bar has also seen the coming and going, often thanks to fire, of a series of structures including the Opera House, the Union Hall (pictured), a drug store, and assorted bars and other establishments. Perhaps these fires were difficult to fight because of the rough topography over which Superior is spread, known as Horse Thief Canyon. The town is known locally as "Little Siberia" – although the average temperature is moderate, it can reach extremes of 20 to 40 degrees below zero on a winter night.

Canyon Bar, Superior

Twenty miles north of Thermpolis a weather-battered sign reads: *Shorty's Bar, left at light.* Those used to Wyoming distances have no problem waiting for that light to come and have it be the only light in town. It leads to Shorty's, run by "Miss Kitty." Bar regulars are used to strangers coming in needing directions to the Dinosaur Museum, which is nearby but hard to find. According to the locals, the green dinosaur tracks painted on city streets to show the way to the museum were allowed to fade. Apparently they too closely resembled marijuana leaves. Altough no dinosaurs dwell there, Shorty's is a great place to chat about local rodeo legends.

Limestone hot spring formation in Hot Springs State Park (top). While there is a world-famous dinosaur quarry up the road a few miles from Shorty's, there is another very interesting dinosaur graveyard much closer (above).

Silver Sage Saloon, Shoshoni

The Silver Sage Saloon in Shoshoni is sometimes overshadowed by the famed Yellowstone Drug with its renowned shakes and malts. The Silver Sage offers refreshment, too, and is a handy stop for folks heading north to scenic Wind River Canyon or to Boysen Reservoir for fishing or boating. Holly and Keith and their Pomeranian dog greet visitors to the bar. A stuffed black bear stood (safely chained) in a sort of bear box on the sidewalk in front of the door. He has since been brought inside for safekeeping.

Frannie Bar, Frannie

The town of Frannie straddles Big Horn and Park counties and almost reaches the Montana state line. The town was named after Frannie Morris, whose father started the post office. She was said to have been a performer in Buffalo Bill Cody's Wild West Show. Customers of the Frannie Bar sometimes include bar tourist and bar tour dogs like Spike.

Cactus Tree Pub, Granger

Granger started life as a stage stop garrisoned to protect travelers from Indians. It has also been a stop on the Pony Express and for the Union Pacific Railroad. Before any of that happened, this site on the banks of the Blacks Fork was a welcome rendezvous spot for hot and thirsty mountain men. The hot and thirsty gather today in the comfort of the Cactus Tree Pub, recently renamed Antelope Crossing.

Proprietors Ed and Jessica's customers include local oil field workers, miners, ranchers, and seasonal sheep herders from Mexico, Peru, and Chile.

Typical badland formations in the high desert north of Granger (below) and ruins of the Pony Express Station in Granger (right).

Shamrock Saloon, Sybille Canyon

Folks who live in the Sybille Canyon area are usually busy with ranching and other work. Sometimes they take time off to visit the Shamrock Saloon, which sits just east of the narrow canyon. The road through the canyon was once much narrower, but in recent years it has been widened and straightened to

accommodate modern motor vehicle traffic. "Be careful of our deer," is a common way for bar regulars to say so long to visitors headed out at dusk. Bar proprietor Laura organizes old-time-music jam sessions and barbecue parties in summer, when the living in the canyon is a bit easier than in the cold, icy, winter months.

Virginian Hotel, Medicine Bow

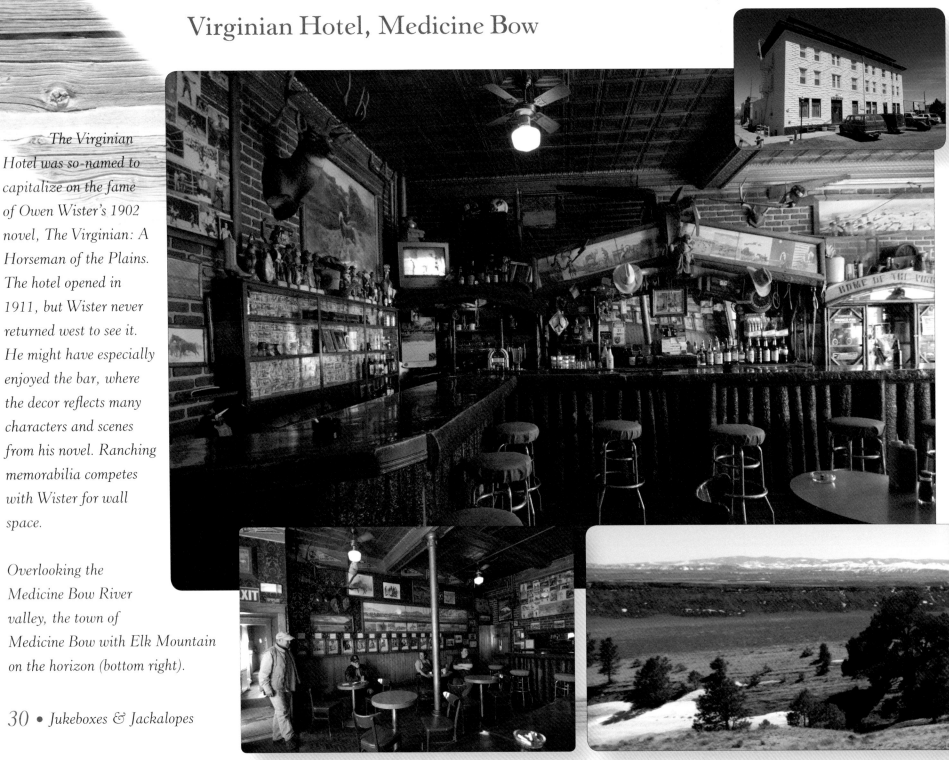

The Virginian Hotel was so-named to capitalize on the fame of Owen Wister's 1902 novel, The Virginian: A Horseman of the Plains. The hotel opened in 1911, but Wister never returned west to see it. He might have especially enjoyed the bar, where the decor reflects many characters and scenes from his novel. Ranching memorabilia competes with Wister for wall space.

Overlooking the Medicine Bow River valley, the town of Medicine Bow with Elk Mountain on the horizon (bottom right).

Diplodicus Bar, Medicine Bow

Known locally as The Dip, this bar was named for the Jurassic-era fossil of a diplodicus dinosaur found in nearby Como Bluff. The bar top is made from richly colored Wyoming jade (nephrite), the state's official gemstone. Hand-painted local scenes by proprietor Bill Bennett adorn the walls, ceiling, and furniture, along with his wood carvings and other art made by his wife, JoAnne.

Invasion Bar, Kaycee

The Invasion Bar and the Hole in the Wall Bar once sat side by side. After a raging thunderstorm in 2002, floodwaters from the Middle Fork of the Powder River raced through Kaycee. Many houses and businesses were damaged or destroyed, including the Hole in the Wall, which sailed down Nolan Avenue and left a hole in the ground next to the Invasion. Now the Hole in the Wall has a new home in a converted gas station, and all is well.

Hole in the Wall Bar, Kaycee

The Hole in the Wall Bar was named in honor of the site where Butch Cassidy and other outlaws hid quite effectively from lawmen. The Invasion Bar's name refers to the Johnson

County Wars, when small ranchers and homesteaders were "invaded" by big cattle interests and their hired Texas gunmen, in 1892.

Hole-in-the-Wall country still takes effort to reach (left).

Dixon Club, Dixon

Dixon sits between Savery to the east and Baggs to the west. Highway 70 over the Sierra Madre range to the east is closed seasonally, so this section of Wyoming sees mostly local traffic in winter and only slightly more traffic at other times of the year. Coming down the slope from the east, travelers progress from lush mountain valley terrain to the increasingly arid Sand Creek region. Baggs, to Dixon's west, is the gateway to the southern Red Desert and Adobe Town area. Ranchers, energy workers, and others visit the Dixon Club for supper and socializing.

Desert Bar, Wamsutter

Once a lonely outpost in the high Red Desert, Wamsutter is now growing rapidly, housing people who work for local gas and oil field exploration companies. The Desert Bar has long been shelter for locals and visitors alike. Now the newer residents of Wamsutter keep the Desert Bar busy. The handpainted Western facade is as unpretentious as the bar's interior. Collages of cowboys and other Western characters, made from arrowheads and pieces of flint tools, decorate walls above the booths.

The Little Snake River valley (below center).

Rosie's Bar, Diamondville

Not to give away a lady's exact age, but Rosie is in her eighties now and has lived in this home/bar since she was two years old. Of course, she didn't operate it herself when she was a toddler, but she and her family have quite a few tales to tell about Diamondville and Rosie's Bar. She knows the stories of the local mines and the men who worked them. Here, she pauses for a Coke and a cigarette during a hard few days of tidying up the bar. Her grandson, Chris, gives her a hand.

The Diamondville Saloon survived Prohibition by becoming a pool hall. "Smokehouse" was added to the name because of the thick smoke surrounding the tables. The building has since become a private museum.

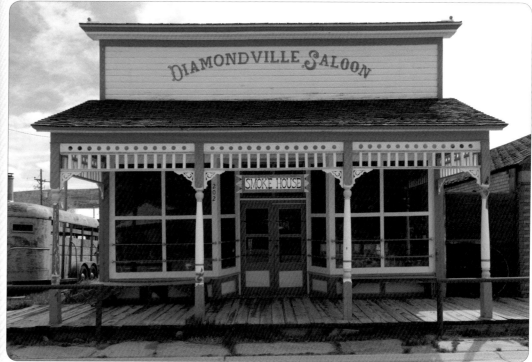

Jim Bridger Club, Fort Bridger

Bridger Valley and Wasatch Mountains (below).

A scattering of small communities nestle in the Bridger Valley, one of the few places in Wyoming where towns are close together. Of the several gathering spots in the Valley, the Jim Bridger Club is one of the most popular. It is just a few blocks away from historic Fort Bridger. Conversation in this bar, more often than not, centers on plans for the Mountain Man Rendezvous, which happens here each Labor Day weekend and brings thousands of visitors to town.

Albany Bar, Cheyenne

The building housing the Albany Bar was built around 1900 as a hotel with rooms upstairs and a lobby, restaurant, and bar on the main level. It stood a block away from the Cheyenne Club, which was built in 1881 as an exclusive social club for cattle barons. Because the Albany sits across the street from the Union Pacific Depot, it has long attracted railroaders and travelers as customers. Now that the Depot has been converted into a museum, the Albany Bar serves many tourists visiting the site, along with the usual local customers.

Arvada Bar, Arvada

An artesian spring richly infused with natural gas once flowed in Arvada. Local residents were known to amuse visitors by striking matches and setting fire to glasses of the spring water. Now residents amuse themselves at the Arvada Bar, and families can visit for meals eaten under the watchful gaze of fishing and hunting trophies. Although the words "Arvada Bar" have abandoned "The" on the building's facade, the Hamm's sign testifies to the fact that it is a bar.

Split Rock Bar, Jeffrey City

The Split Rock Bar & Cafe is named after Split Rock, a formation east of here that was a landmark for travelers on the emigrant trails. Jeffrey City, originally called Home on the Range, has been the center of some of Wyoming's most dramatic boom and bust phases. The Split Rock Bar & Cafe is one of the few businesses still open, although the uranium mining that created the boom may come back and bring the town with it.

Sweetwater Station, Sweetwater River Crossing

Sweetwater Station was established in 1862. It has been, among other things, a telegraph relay station, a military supply base, and a Pony Express station. It was an essential rest stop for travelers near Independence Rock and the Sweeetwater River Crossing along the Oregon Trail. In 1926 it kept up with the times and became a gas station. It has stayed in the same family for several generations since that time, and its bar and convenience store are welcome sites, and sights, for modern travelers.

Elkhorn Bar, Bondurant

Bondurant is a town of 100 residents that takes up a lot of space, strewn as it is along narrow Hoback Canyon on the banks of the Hoback River. Bondurant's elevation of 6588 feet isn't high by Wyoming standards but seems so as one starts the plunge down the canyon into Jackson Hole. Bar regulars have kept a photo album for years, showing results of their hunts in the nearby Gros Ventre or Wyoming ranges. Sometimes the deceased wildlife shows up in the bar, if only briefly.

Bighorn Sheep are some of the residents of Hoback Canyon

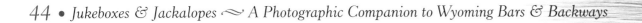

Edelweiss Bar, Clark

Edelweiss is a small, white, perennial flower that grows high up in the Alps. The mountain country around Yellowstone National Park conjurs visions of those European mountains, so it is little wonder that the Edelweiss's owners chose that name for their bar. Artwork in the bar depicts mountain scenes of the sort that attracted the likes of writer Ernest Hemingway to the area in the late 1920s. Clark, the town and the river, were named for William Clark, co-captain of the Corps of Discovery.

Badger Basin, near Clark (right).

Rowdy's Spirits & Bait, Hyattville

Human habitation and visitation in this area of north central Wyoming go back 10,000 years. Nearby Medicine Lodge Creek Valley was their destination then and still is today. But an additional modern comfort is available now to today's visitors to Hyattville and the Medicine Lodge State Archaelogical Site: Rowdy's Spirits & Bait (now known as the Hyattville Bar).

Red rocks of the Chugwater formation along the Red Gulch/Alkali Scenic Backway (below).

Woods Landing Bar, Woods Landing

Mr. Woods carried freight from a landing at this spot on the Big Laramie River to North Park, Colorado. He later opened a saloon on the site for stage drivers and tie hacks. His wife was a great cook, so the saying went that no one left hungry when visiting Woods Landing. The current resort was developed in the 1920s. The dance floor was built of hand-grooved logs on top of 24 boxcar springs. The bar has become locally famous for weekend dances and was listed on the National Register of Historic Places in 1986.

Longbranch Saloon, Hawk Springs

The town of Hawk Springs has few businesses and only one bar/restaurant. Recently, that number has been reduced to zero, thanks to a fire that destroyed the Longbranch Saloon. However, the owners plan to rebuild this regionally popular bar, live music venue, and steak-house. Visiting goose and pheasant hunters, along with fishermen, will await that day as eagerly as locals and passing bikers on their way to the motorcycle rally in Sturgis, South Dakota.

Yoder Bar, Yoder

What the Yoder Bar lacks in exterior beauty, it makes up for on the inside. Individual local artists, perhaps inspired by Michelangelo's Sistine Chapel ceiling, have painted every section of the acoustical tile ceiling above the horseshoe-shaped bar.

Fields of winter wheat in Goshen Hole (below).

Silver Dollar Bar, Jackson

The Silver Dollar Bar was minted in 1950. It resides in the Wort Hotel, which was completed in 1941 by the Charles Wort family, who homesteaded here. The Silver Dollar Bar was constructed by a German cabinet maker. He used 2,032 uncirculated silver dollars from the Federal Reserve Bank in Denver to give a unique look to the bar's top. Fire threatened to destroy the hotel and bar in 1980, collapsing the roof, and indeed it was closed for awhile. It reopened in 1981, much to the joy of regular customers and tourists, who visit Jackson Hole in ever-increasing numbers.

Mount Moran, the Teton Mountain Range along the Snake River at Moran Junction (left).

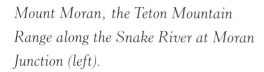

Million Dollar Cowboy Bar, Jackson

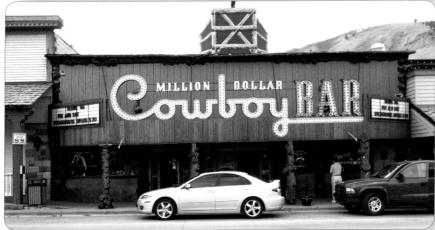

1937 was a good year for folks who enjoy socializing in bars. It was the year Prohibition was repealed, and the first liquor license awarded in Wyoming went to Ben Goe, the owner of what was then called the Cowboy Bar. It was renamed the Milllion Dollar Cowboy Bar when it was purchased in the mid-1940s by Preston Parkinson. In a familiar story of bar fires, the bar was nearly destroyed in 1953 by a gas explosion in the basement. Parkinson rebuilt and the bar carried on. It was later sold to Ron Schultz, Bud Jensen, and Cliff Poindexter, who installed the famous saddle-seat bar stools. Since 1988 the bar has been owned by Art & Carol Andersen and Hagan & Roger Dudley. The bar competes for visitors by being one of the best live music venues in the area and by creating a traditional Western ambience.

Bill's day the town has changed, and so has the hotel. His original saloon, with its cherry back bar, is now the dining area. The current bar, known as the Silver Saddle Saloon, contains Buffalo Bill memorabilia, including one of his saddles. During summer, the place is packed with visitors who step out on the hotel's porch to witness staged gunfights. In winter, it provides a charming refuge for locals and visitors to the Park.

Cody is tourist heaven (in summertime, especially) for a few very good reasons. The first is its proximity to Yellowstone National Park and other national forests and wilderness areas. Another reason is that Buffalo Bill Cody planned it that way when he founded the town in 1895, and his plan worked. One step in his plan to make Cody a destination town was to build a fine hotel, which he did, and named it for his daughter, Irma. Since Buffalo

Looking toward Shell Canyon and the Wind River Mountains from the Red Gulch Scenic Backway south of Greybull.

Smokehouse Saloon, Greybull

An antique back bar anchors the furnishings of this friendly regulars' bar. A large photograph of a branding scene, one in a series taken in the 1930s by Charles Belden, hangs on the opposite wall, surrounded by artwork and other photos of Western scenes. And of course, mounted wildlife trophies watch the daily proceedings from their perches along the walls.

Lost Bar, Lost Springs

"Get lost in Lost Springs," the locals always say. At least that's what a town souvenir reads. The "Bar" sign can be seen from US Highway 18/20, helping people not get lost on their way to town. One reason people venture off the highway is to photograph the sign that proclaims the population of Lost Springs to be 1. The Lost Bar is openly primarily during hunting season in the fall. The folks at the Lost Springs store offer interesting antiques, knick-knacks, and ironically, directions to hidden spots in the Thunder Basin National Grassland.

Steelman's Brite Spot, Hiland

The social scene in Hiland, population 10, is mainly focused on the Brite Spot. A convenience store brings travelers into the mix, and when they enter the bar, things can get crowded. The bar in the Brite Spot is one of the smallest in Wyoming: it didn't take long for customers to cover the walls with business cards and dollar bills commemorating their visit. A guitar kept behind the bar breaks the ice between newcomers and locals, and sometimes even full-scale jam sessions are known to break out.

Atlantic City Mercantile, Atlantic City

Nestled in South Pass, Atlantic City is known for its historic gold mines, but the origin of the town's name is disputed. Regardless, the Mercantile, or "The Merc," as it is known, was built in 1893 and was no doubt heavily visited by the town's population, which once reached more than 2,000. Now the 28 hardy year-round residents, additional summer dwellers, and tourists to historic mines and emigrant Mormon sites keep the bar and restaurant busy. The bar was made by Brunswick-Balke-Collender Co., in the early 1900s. It was first used in Hudson, Wyoming, and moved to Atlantic City in 1967. In 1985, the building was added to the National Register of Historic Places.

Miner's Grubstake Saloon, Atlantic City

Grubstake (noun, 1863): Supplies or funds furnished a mining prospector on promise of a share of his discoveries. The Miner's Grubstake is just a stone's throw from the Merc, and both supply the denizens of Atlantic City with the supplies they need for a meal or evening out, no prospecting required.

...ed Canyon situated at the southern end ... the Wind River Mountains between ...tlantic City and Lander (left).

Ponderosa Saloon, Hulett

Devils Tower National Monument, also known as Bear Lodge, is the hub in the wheel of several small towns in northeast Wyoming. The nation's first national monument, Devils Tower stands 1,280 feet above the Belle Fouche River valley. The town of Hulett, with its approximately 500 residents, swells to several times that size during the Sturgis motorcycle rally. Bikers take a break from the throngs of Harley riders in the Black Hills of South Dakota for some quiet time in Hulett. At the Ponderosa Bar, paintings by area artists share space with ranch memorabilia.

The Bighorn Mountains shimmer above Buffalo
on a June afternoon (far bottom right).

Occidental Saloon, Buffalo

A cast of western characters, from Butch Cassidy and the Sundance Kid to Calamity Jane to Buffalo Bill Cody, have stayed at the Occidental Hotel. We can only guess if they raised a glass in the Occidental Saloon or dined in the adjoining Virginian restaurant. Owen Wister, who wrote the novel by that name, stopped there often. Perhaps the people who visit the bar today discuss the fine points of western literature during happy hour.

Dad's Bar & Steakhouse, Thayne

The Star Valley was named by Mormon settler Moses Thatcher in 1870. He proclaimed it was the star of valleys. Tiny ranching towns dot the area, including Thayne, home of Dad's Bar & Steakhouse. Dad's has long been the headquarters for cutter racing, or quarter horse racing, a winter sport in which a rider is pulled in a sleigh mounted on skis. As they say in town, "We're not crazy – we're in Thayne!"

Livestock graze on the rich grasses of agriculture-loving Star Valley.

Shelly's Cowboy Bar, Afton

Afton was named by Mormon settlers from Scotland after this line from a Robert Burns poem, "flow gently, Sweet Afton." The stream in Wyoming was anything but gentle, so the naming was a bit of an irony. The largest town in Star Valley, Afton boasts several bars, but Shelly's has some of the most interesting exterior signage in western Wyoming.

Bear Pit Lounge, Old Faithful Inn, Yellowstone National Park

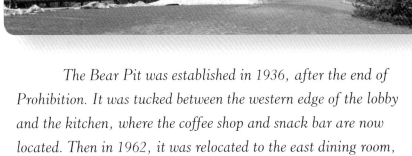

The Bear Pit was established in 1936, after the end of Prohibition. It was tucked between the western edge of the lobby and the kitchen, where the coffee shop and snack bar are now located. Then in 1962, it was relocated to the east dining room, where it remains today.

The etched panels were designed by Chicago cartoonist Walter Oehrle. They fancifully represent the wildlife who reside in the park including a bighorn sheep waiter, a pelican guest, bartending bears, and dancing moose.

Fanciful etched glass panel in Bear Pit Bar (left), Old Faithful Inn (above) and craftsman period styled Bear Pit Bar (right).

Bear Pit Lounge, Old Faithful Inn, Yellowstone National Park

The seven-story tall log lobby and free standing stone fireplace of the Old Faithful Inn (far left); early 1900s Haynes postcard of Artist Point, Grand Canyon of the Yellowstone River (above); Yellowstone Lake in early June (left); Old Faithful geyser basin (top).

Leiterville Country Club, Leiter

A "club" for residents of the country around Leiter, the Leiterville Country Club features a cafe in the front and the bar, Joe's Place, in back. Outdoor tables fashioned from wooden cable spools adorn the patio. The Country Club has a post office and offers a few motel rooms for passersby. Leiter forms one fourth of Wyoming's "UCLA" district: Ucross, Clearmont, Leiter, and Arvada.

Spotted Horse Saloon, Spotted Horse

A life-sized fiberglass spotted horse welcomes travelers and locals to stop in to Spotted Horse, population 2, and shoot a game of pool. Spotted Horse is an oasis in the high, dry country of the Powder River Basin. It was once a post office – that's why it remains on the Wyoming highway map.

Location Bar, La Barge

Oil and natural gas drilling has long been a mainstay of La Barge, through numerous booms and busts. Anyone interested in how workers extract oil and gas should visit the bar and admire the very large, heavy-duty drill bits and related items on display there. La Barge is just north of Names Hill, a spot along the Sublette Cutoff of the Oregon Trail. Travelers scratched their names and dates as they passed this spot on their way to greener pastures. Names date back as far as 1827; Native American petroglyphs are also present in the area.

The Green River in La Barge (left).

Esterbrook Bar, Esterbrook

If you can reach the Esterbrook Bar, you deserve whatever cold beverages or giant burgers await you there. Located in a truly rugged section of the Laramie Range, the Esterbrook Bar is best reached by four-wheel-drive vehicle or snowmobile. The orginial part of the bar was built in the early 1900s, with other portions added on as the fancy struck. Kenny the bartender is a descendant of the family who built the bar and has worked for the new owners, on and off, for many years. He can tell you the best Forest Service roads to follow back to Wheatland, Douglas, or Rock River.

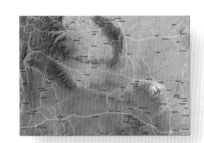

This homestead nestles in a granite canyon near Laramie Peak, along one of the many scenic approaches to Esterbrook.

Bozeman Trail Saloon, Big Horn

To those who have visited the Bozeman Trail Saloon before the kitchen fire, these interior images may seem foreign. The owners turned potential calamity into a chance to remodel the bar, complete with bamboo flooring and a "Smurf" pool table. Among the items salvaged are the back bar and mirror. The town of Big Horn was along the Bozeman Trail from the Platte River to Montana, east of the mountain range. The trail was laid out and protected by the government in violation of treaties with Native Americans.

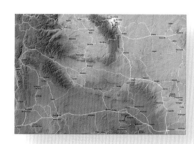

Wonder Bar, Casper

Photo of the Wonder Bar from an earlier, horsier time.

The Wonder Bar proclaims itself to be world famous, and so it may be. It certainly is famous in central Wyoming and is "the place to go" that locals recommend when tourists come to town. Pressed tin ceilings and horse & rider decor complement the unwind-after-work atmosphere. The Wonder Bar, now complete with micro-brew and restaurant, has been a mainstay in Casper since 1934.

Old Western Saloon, Glendo

Proof of the truism that a book cannot be judged by its cover is the Old Western Saloon. Its modest exterior belies the creatively decorated surfaces and rich atmosphere found inside. The bar lore includes a story of the back bar being brought to the West from Italy in the 1800s. After doing a stint in Deadwood, S.D., it was moved to this saloon.

Glendo Reservoir is particularly high after a wet spring, and some of its campsites and trees are under water.

Along the trail between Wyarno and Ucross.

Wyarno Bar & Grill, Wyarno

Arno is a river in Italy – what better name to give a railroad station in Wyoming, thus, Wyarno. This bar, grill, and post office stands alone at the end of a paved road east of Sheridan. A gravel road eventually leads to the "U" in UCLA: Ucross, home of the Ucross Foundation. Ucross no longer has a bar, so the artists and writers in residency there often blend with the local residents and seasonal hunters.

Bear Tree Tavern, Centennial

This former gold mining town at the foot of the Snowy Range Mountains was founded in 1876, thus the name. Coincidentally, the population sign never various from its count of 100 residents. The Bear Tree Tavern is one of several bars in town catering to residents of Centennial and of Laramie 25 miles to the east, along with scores of hikers, cyclists, skiers, and snowmobilers who trudge up and down the Scenic Byway. In the summer, the tavern hosts outdoor music festivals on its back lawn while music fans dodge hummingbirds and wandering resident dogs.

Centennial Valley in late summer (below right).

Trading Post Saloon, Centennial

The Trading Post stands at 8,000 feet and offers visitors many ways to recover from the effects of altitude. For starters, a steakhouse offers dinner, prominently featuring steak. A dance floor and stage are the scene of weekend music. On some nights, the restaurant serves as the opening act to a community dinner theatre. After dining, patrons remove to the small theatre space at the west end of the building. A small art gallery is housed near the rear of the building, and a redwood deck is often full in summer with patrons enjoying views of Sheep Mountain and the Centennial Valley. The deck allows access to the saloon, which occupies the east side of the building.

Wildflowers adorn Libby Flats, with Medicine Bow peak in view.

Butch's Place, Kirby

Butch's Place uses burgers and beer to satisfy the appetites of the town's 50-some-odd residents. It is also a welcome site for those recreating or working on the massive area of BLM lands spanning miles in all directions from town.

Blue Mesa in the Big Horn Basin (below).

Pete's Roc N Rye Club, Evanston

Residents of Evanston and nearby communities still tell tales of evenings dancing and having a good time at the Roc N Rye Club. That was back when the club was a popular stop along the Lincoln Highway. Interstate 80, with its high speed traffic, seems to have left Pete's to another time. Rumor has it that the place is still open on rare occasions. Find the driveway in by taking the access road, rather than the interstate.

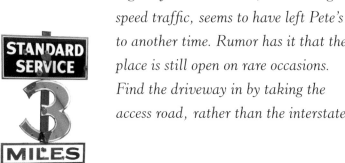

Wolf Hotel & Bar, Saratoga

The town of Saratoga was named for Saratoga Springs, New York. It is a Wyoming resort due to its hot mineral springs pools, trout-laden North Platte River, and spots like the Wolf Hotel & Bar. The Wolf opened in 1893 for travelers attracted to the mineral springs. The rooms have been restored to their original charm, but one can imagine they are now much more comfortable. The bar is adorned with Georgia pine and many noteworthy decorations from marlin to swizzle-sticks.

Rustic Bar, Saratoga

While the bar at the Wolf Hotel is popular with locals and visitors to Saratoga alike, the Rustic is better known as the locals' hangout. A realistic tableau of stuffed mountain lions skirmishing over their unfortunate prey and various other heads and horns on display make great conversation starters.

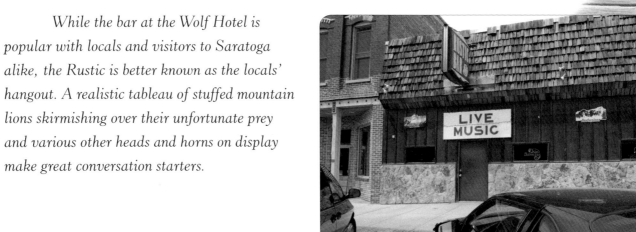

Bear Trap Bar, Riverside

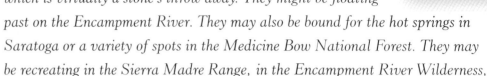

Situated side by side in the town of Riverside, the Bear Trap and Mangy Moose Saloon accommodate various passersby. People come by car on their way to Encampment, which is virtually a stone's throw away. They might be floating past on the Encampment River. They may also be bound for the hot springs in Saratoga or a variety of spots in the Medicine Bow National Forest. They may be recreating in the Sierra Madre Range, in the Encampment River Wilderness,

Mangy Moose Saloon, Riverside

or taking in the sights at the Grand Encampment Museum. Or, they may have "fallen off" the Continental Divide National Scenic Trail that passes near here. Both watering holes provide provisions for long-range hikers on the trail, as well as places to wash up, rest up, and collect mail. The town of Riverside was originally founded in the 1850s as a rendezvous spot for whites and Native Americans; Encampment was founded in the 1890s primarily as a copper mining town.

Lander Bar, Lander

The Lander area has long been a Wyoming crossroads, and in modern times, the story is stll the same. The town's usually moderate weather and proximity to the Wind River Mountains has attracted an outdoors school and a Catholic college to join the ranks of local ranchers, Native Americans, and other folks seeking a place to settle. Often they wind up together in the Lander Bar, making it one of Wyoming's top spots for people-watching.